THAMES·VALLEY

THE
BRITISH
YEARS: 1915-1920

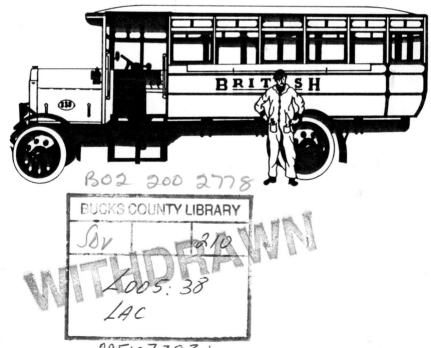

Written and published by PAUL LACEY

ISBN 0 9510739 3 1

Other titles by the author:

The Independent Bus & Coach Operators of the Newbury Area, 1919-1932   *£4.95* *

A History of Newbury & District Motor Services Ltd., 1932-1952   *£6.75*

A History of the Penn Bus Company, 1920-1935   *£2.50*

*Available from good bookshops, or direct from the above address (*not direct now)*

ACKNOWLEDGEMENTS

A history such as this is like a jigsaw puzzle where pieces turn up in random order and, frustratingly, some are never found. Over the past 22 years I have endeavoured to assemble as much of the picture as possible, and to that end I have contacted numerous people and organisations. To each of those who have responded to my enquiries I say "thank you", no matter how small their contribution may have seemed.

Some sources do, however, require a special mention : the staff of the Berkshire Record Office; the Reference/Local Studies Sections of the libraries of Berkshire and its borders; and the editors of the local newspapers.

However, this story would undoubtably have been a duller one had it not been enlightened by the first-hand experiences of those who were involved with the enterprise. Mr T A G Homer (son of T Graham Homer) kindly made available his family archives (including roll-film negatives of the early days and his father's own potted history of the period), whilst much detail came to light over the years during interviews with Charlie Hampton, Frank Williams, Alf Waterman, Charles Bridgewater, Arthur ('Nobby') Clarke and others amongst the early employees.

In conclusion, I would like to dedicate this book to the memory of all those men and women who kept the 'British' and 'Thames Valley' buses going during those pioneering days.

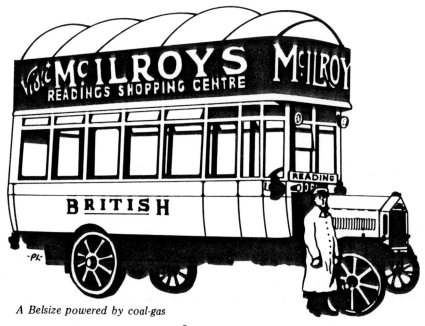

A Belsize powered by coal-gas

During the very early years of the 20th Century the tramway- owning British Electric Traction Co. Ltd. foresaw that the motorbus had a future, both as a feeder to the tramways (without the construction costs of additional lines), and as a means of developing new operations outside the urban areas.

In acknowledgement of this aspect of forward thinking BET set up the British Automobile Development Co. Ltd. in 1905, with the dual aims of developing suitable vehicles (at the associated Brush Electrical Engineering works at Loughborough) and to initiate new bus operations. The BAD changed its name to the British Automobile Traction Co. Ltd. in 1912 and, although some of the early operations proved troublesome (due in the main to the unreliability of those early vehicles and the poor condition of the roads), the Company nonetheless persevered and set up a number of new bus operations in various parts of the country.

The BAT headquarters were at the BET offices at 88 Kingsway in London, whilst Emile Garcke (founder of BET) and his son (Sidney) both resided at Ditton House, Pinkneys Green, near Maidenhead in Berkshire. Sidney had been very involved with the bus developments of the business and had learnt much about both the advantages and the pitfalls of motorbus operation. It was only natural therefore that Sidney should duly recognise the potential for bus services in the mid-Thames valley area and to take the setting up of such a Branch under his own wing.

Amongst the engineers already known to Sidney Garcke was another young man of almost the same age named T. Graham Homer, with whom he often played tennis. Homer had been born in 1888 the son of a mining engineer and had trained at the Crompton works at Chelmsford as an electrical engineer, subsequently taking up several posts involved in railed traction. In 1911 he and his wife left for Canada where he was involved in the development of the hydro-electric power plant at St. Timothee on the St. Lawrence River. Whilst in Canada they had a son, but the harsh winters did not appeal to them, so not too much was required to urge then back to Britain. Such an opportunity did indeed arise in the very grip of the winter months of early 1915, when Homer's mother relayed to him an offer from Sidney Garcke for him to take up the post of Engineer and Manager of the proposed new Branch being set up in the Thames valley. The initial news was sent by telegram to Canada, and the reply was a short but jubilant 'Hooray. Send £15 for fare!' - and the start of a 29 year career as head of the new venture was set to begin.

As soon as Graham Homer had returned to Britain he was sent to study the BAT operations at Camden Town, Birmingham and Deal as part of his induction into his new role. Although he lacked any formal management training, he was a good (if at times a little autocratic) organiser and was full of enthusiasm for the project ahead.

Sidney Garcke made public the proposed new venture during March 1915, announcing the intention of starting with a service between Maidenhead, Reading and Streatley, which would be followed by the opening up of a route between Reading and Newbury. However, there

4

were a number of matters that required attention before services could actually commence, the situation being made all the more difficult by the over-riding needs of the military due to the First World War.

Indeed, the military requisitioning of bus chassis for use as lorries had already decimated the BAT operations across the country, one of the locations affected being the small operation based on Banbury. In order to assist with the new venture, the small Banbury staff (consisting of foreman Bob Hepburn, driver Owen Fox, conductor Charlie Hampton, plus the chief clerk) were all transferred to Reading.

Bob Hepburn was a Scot and, most fortunately for BAT and Mr Homer, an excellent mechanic who did his utmost to overcome the often troublesome ways of the early buses. He spent the remainder of his working life with the Reading firm, latterly as Works Super- intendant, until his death in 1950. Conductor Charlie Hampton also remained at Reading throughout his working life (though he soon transferred to the driving seat when he was old enough), and was still a familiar sight helping out part-time with parcels etc. around Reading bus station well after he reached retirement age in the late 1960's.

Premises for the new Branch were secured in Reading during March 1915 and took the form of Nos. 113-117 Caversham Road, situated about 1/2 a mile from the town centre. The properties consisted of a shop with living accommodation over it (Nos. 115-117) and a sizeable yard and garage which was reached through an extrance formed by the demolition of No. 113. The garage and yard had latterly been occupied by William Vincent & Son, pioneer motor engineers of Reading, and had been used to house their taxi fleet. As acquired the garage provided covered accommodation for 9 buses, whilst the yard area could take many more. Initially the rooms above the shop were used to provide temporary lodgings for the small band of employees assembled at the outset, but later that summer No. 117 was leased out to another user.

Graham Homer and Bob Hepburn equipped the garage with whatever plant and tools they could manage to obtain, whilst Charlie Hampton and Owen Fox helped survey the proposed routes and develop timetables etc. However, the Branch still lacked any vehicles with which to start its operations, as the order placed by BAT with Thornycrofts of Basingstoke for 20 J-type chassis had remained unfulfilled due to the whole of the works production being taken by the War Department. With little immediate hope of any improvement to that situation. BAT made arrangements for 2 Leyland single-deck buses to be transferred to Reading from the 'Barnsley & District' fleet. Homer and Hepburn collected the vehicles from Barnsley, but first had to take them to Birch Bros. at Kentish Town for overhaul and repainting due to their poor state of repair. Homer was also rather concerned about the prospects of maintaining the proposed service without any spare buses, and his representations soon resulted in the transfer down from Barnsley of the 3 other members of that particular batch of Leylands.

The 5 buses were all of the 40hp S8 type delivered new in May 1913, and they carried Brush 27-seat front-entrance saloon bodies incorporating such refinements as electric lighting and cushioned seating. The driver was largely protected from the elements by a full-height windscreen, whilst there were 2 rows of seats with open body sides towards the front of the vehicle. The side windows could be removed for better ventilation in good weather and, although already 2 years old, the buses were better from the passengers point of view than anything then to be found in the Capital. Registered HE 8 to HE 12, the batch passed through the Birch workshops between June and early August 1915 and were finished in the Saxon Green 'British' livery with large gold fleetnames and fully lined-out lower panels.

Once the matter of rolling stock had been resolved it was possible to inaugurate the operations, and Saturday 31st July 1915 was the date chosen for the commencement of a service from Reading to Maidenhead and Streatley. To whet the public's appetite for the new venture Graham Homer submitted a small write-up and a posed photograph of Bob Hepburn and HE 12 at the 'Bull' in Streatley for inclusion in the 'Berkshire Chronicle' published the day before the service started.

The route was operated by Reading-based buses and the first left for Streatley at 7.20 am and the other for Maidenhead at 7.40 am. The 2 cars (HE 11 and 12 at first) ran back and forth over the whole route between Maidenhead and Streatley for the rest of the day, and passengers could travel the whole length of the route without having to change bus. The route ran from the 'Bear Hotel' at Maidenhead and along the Bath Road through Maidenhead Thicket, Littlewick Green, Knowl Hill and Twyford before turning off that famous highway to pass through Sonning village and over the Thames into Oxfordshire. From there it continued its way via Play Hatch and Caversham before returning into Berkshire over Caversham Bridge to enter Reading past the Branch office and on to the main stop at St. Mary's Butts. Here the buses halted for 5 minutes before the journey was resumed via Tilehurst, Purley, Pangbourne and Basildon and on to the 'Bull' at Streatley.

Although the bus service paralleled some existing rail links, it was particularly useful to those numerous people who were not conveniently situated for the stations. At 23 ^{1}/2 miles the route was unusually long for a pioneering service at that time, and the 2 buses each travelled over 110 miles each day.

When the Reading Branch commenced its operations motorised public transport was virtually unknown in the area. Only Edwin Venn-Brown of Henley was running a regular 'bus' service into Reading (using his 'Venture' charabanc), whilst other facilities were limited to the carriers services (few of which had progressed to motor vehicles by that date). Also, only one motorised charabanc was on offer in Reading (that being Dennis DP 1225 of John Humphries of the 'Lodge Hotel'), but even that was not heard of after the 1915 season.

Not that the local roads made such operations particularly easy (or comfortable!), as even the Bath Road was a patchwork of loose gravel and potholes when the 'British' buses first turned their wheels upon it. Indeed,

6

the venture was a bold one to undertake, but fortunately the sun shone long and hot that summer and the public were tempted to sample the new facility in good numbers. Particularly popular were the 'outside' seats towards the front of the bus, where both fresh air and a good view of the road ahead could be enjoyed. The buses shared the roads with very little other traffic, private motoring having been severely curtailed by the war, and the most widespread alternative means of personal transport was still the bicycle.

However, by far the most daunting task facing Graham Homer in 1915 was the provision of crews for the buses. Initially the only licenced drivers were Owen Fox, Bob Hepburn and Homer himself, but shortly afterwards others were recruited and trained from the very limited pool of local men not required for military service or engaged on war work. Any thought of employing male conductors was basically out of the question, and it was left to the efforts of a hardworking 45 women to cover those duties from the summer of 1915 until 1920, when the last of the 'lady conductors' (they were never referred to as 'conductresses' at the Branch) were ousted by the recruitment of men. Occasionally the situation became so desperate that drivers had to be borrowed from the Camden Town Branch.

Although the proposed route between Reading and Newbury did not materialise as a follow on to the original service, further developments were nonetheless being planned during the summer of 1915 whilst the Reading Branch awaited the delivery of further buses and the recruitment of more drivers.

It should be noted that Mrs. Homer always took a keen interest in the early developments of the local operations, and it became a regular Sunday occupation of the Homers to take a ride out in the Ford car (which had been transferred to Reading in June 1915) in order to survey possible new routes for the buses. Graham Homer had the firm belief that the very presence of a regular bus service would actually stimulate the desirability of living on the roads served and, it must be acknowledged that, as the Metropolitan Railway had created 'metroland', so the coming of the buses lead directly to much of the ribbon-development which was to be found between the towns of east Berkshire.

Another key factor in the success of the Branch would be its relationship with the Local Authorities responsible for the granting of Hackney Carriage licences and the upkeep of the roads. In the case of Reading there was also the fact that the Corporation already had its own tramway network within its boundary and, in order to place matters on a good footing from the start, Sidney Garcke had held discussions with the Corporation at an early stage to allay any fears that the municipal operator might have about the arrival of the buses. It was therefore agreed that 'British' would charge a higher 'protective' fare for passengers whose journey was wholly within the borough, and this arrangement was later extended to include routes sharing the same roads as the RCT buses when they duly started after the war.

The other major Local Authorities exercising powers to control Hackney Carriages in Berkshire were Windsor and Maidenhead, but neither gave any real cause for concern, generally limiting their activities to the stipulation of stopping points and routes taken within their areas. Outside of the towns the buses would stop virtually anywhere, and in doing so they offered a very convenient and often door-to-door service. The buses did, of course, bring much needed additional trade to the towns, whilst villagers were now able to have a wider choice of leisure activities by making use of the buses.

Mr. Homer was particularly keen to establish further services during the summer months of 1915 but the acquisition of further vehicles was still a problem. There seemed no hope at all of receiving any of the Thornycrofts on order whilst the war continued, so arrangements were made to obtain some Belsize 3-ton lorry chassis instead. This Manchester-built type had already been supplied to the Macclesfield Branch to take the place of Daimlers taken by the War Department and, although they had proved themselves a little troublesome, they were at least very unlikely to be taken by the military.

The Belsizes started to arrive during September 1915 and allowed expansion to take place at last. The Maidenhead, Reading and Streatley route was extended by a further 6 miles on to Wallingford early in October to meet up with the newly-introduced 'City of Oxford' service to Oxford. Very shortly afterwards a new link to Abingdon was formed by introducing some additional journeys between Reading and Wallingford which then ran on for a further 14 miles to Abingdon via Shillingford, Dorchester, Buscot, Clifton Hampden and Culham, and provided another connection with the 'City of Oxford' buses at Abingdon.

The original routing of the pioneer service via Sonning did not, however, survive for long before it was re-routed to bypass Sonning in favour of continuing along the Bath Road. Some compensation was made for the Sonning village residents by the erection of the Branch's first passenger shelter on the main road adjacent to the entrance to the Sonning Golf Club (christened 'Sonning Halt' by the Company). From there the service continued along the Bath Road to enter Reading via Cemetery Junction and Kings Road. The exact date of this alteration has not been ascertained, but both it and the splitting of the service at Reading most likely occurred when the route was extended to Wallingford.

The initial batch of Belsizes consisted of 6 chassis and they were fitted with Tilling rear-entrance bus bodies and registered DP 1655 to 1660. The bodies were apparently secondhand, though only about a year or two old, and had most likely already seen service with another Branch on chassis which had been taken by the military. In all 8 such bodies were sent to Reading, all being 26-seaters by Tilling, but where they emanated from is not known.

Replacement by the Belsizes of the Leylands originally used on the Maidenhead, Reading and Streatley route allowed the latter to be used to pioneer further new routes from Reading - though the proposed Newbury link was still not put into operation.

A new service of some 7 miles length to Riseley Common via Whitley Wood, Shinfield and Swallowfield commenced in October 1915, and the route was extended by a short distance to the Wellington Monument at Heckfield Heath on summer Sundays during the following year in order cater for walkers and picnicers wishing to visit the woods and commons thereabouts.

The Branch also commenced running a bus 4 times a day between Reading and Wokingham on an indirect 12 mile route via Shinfield, Arborfield and Barkham on Friday 22nd October 1915. In connection with this venture Homer had approached Wokingham Borough Council to see if they required the buses to be issued with Hackney Carriage licences to operate in their area and, although the Council had not exercised such powers until then, it decided that such licences would be required. However, as this was a new matter, the buses were allowed to continue running whilst the licences were being dealt with in acknowledgement of the trade brought to the town and the link the service provided with the Cavalry Remount Depot at Arborfield.

The next development to the east of Reading took place on Saturday 18th December 1915, when a service was introduced between Reading and Sunningdale which ran via Loddon Bridge, Wokingham, Bracknell and Ascot and provided 4 journeys per day. One of the routes objectives was to reach out a tentacle to meet the edge of the area in which the BAT-associated 'Aldershot & District' company was expanding and with whom the Reading Branch already had a basic territorial understanding. The 18 mile route linked the market towns of Reading, Wokingham and Bracknell both with each other and with the rural areas between them. The service also much improved access to the military hospital which had been established at the Ascot Racecourse, whilst also making a junction with the bus service of the 'Great Western Railway' to Windsor at Ascot High Street.

Provision for the expanding fleet was met by extending the Caversham Road site to take in additional land in the adjacent Swansea Road which had been acquired in July 1915. However, the lack of a telephone service did cause some problems initially, and several requests for such an installation were refused. Mr. Homer had noticed that a large telegraph pole was actually situated on the Branch premises, and his application to remove it caused enough of a fuss that the desired phone line was soon laid on!

Indeed, the value of the bus services was duly recognised as being of national importance, particularly as the buses at Reading were often involved in the carrying of wounded or convalescent military personnel in addition to the day-to-day task of serving the travelling public.

By the end of December 1915 the buses of the Branch had carried 77,072 passengers and covered 54,236 miles since services had begun at the end of July - the venture having been blessed by a hot summer which lasted well into autumn. However, darker clouds loomed on the horizon, as both the continuing warfare and the hostilities of the British weather were soon to have an effect on the Branch's ability to maintain its operations. ▪

The first of a number of wartime restrictions to affect the buses was the passing of the Restricted Lighting Order, which had been designed to make Britain less vulnerable to airborne attack from Zeppelins. It took effect from January 1916 and meant that the buses could only show sidelights at night - making driving on the dark country roads hazardous and leading to the curtailment of some late evening journeys during the dark months of the year.

The Branch was still determined to expand despite the difficulties faced and, during January 1916, a large site was secured in Maidenhead in order to set up a second centre for operations. The site was occupied by a large old house called 'The Cedars' and which had extensive grounds both to the front and rear of it. Plans for the construction of a garage for about half-a-dozen buses were put before Maidenhead Borough Council during January and gained approval that same month. Much of the house was demolished as it was in poor condition, but the east wing was retained for use as offices. The garage was constructed in widthways fashion across the east/west axis of the site and linked the old east wing with a new building built to house the stores and the garage foreman's office. The construction of the garage allowed for easy extension rearwards into the former garden, whilst a good-sized forecourt was provided in front of the garage but was separated from the road by the retention of much of the grassed area and many of the trees.

The Maidenhead garage continued to be referred to as 'The Cedars' for some time after its new role commenced, but the property was otherwise known as 44 Bridge Street and was situated just a little way eastwards of the town centre towards Maidenhead Bridge on a section of the Bath Road.

Work on the new garage had been completed by March 1916 and, at the end of that month a further pair of Belsizes joined the fleet. Registered DP 1756 and 1757, these chassis received the other 2 Tilling 26-seat bodies mentioned earlier. Their arrival led to the withdrawal from service in April 1916 of Leylands HE 10 and 11. Their exact fate is a little uncertain, but they may well have been the pair of S-types later re-registered as FL 1561 and 1562 by the BET-controlled 'Peterborough Electric Traction' company.

A new service had been opened up early in 1916 from Maidenhead (the 'Bear') to the Canadian Red Cross Hospital which had been set up some 3 miles from the centre of Maidenhead in the grounds of the Astor's Cliveden estate to cope with the war wounded. The route involved a steep climb from the Bath Road to Taplow Court up Berry Hill, and the conductor had to be ready on the platform with a wooden chock in case the bus should roll back - one lady conductor unfortunately losing several of her fingers during such a manouvre.

10

The exact date of the introduction of the Cliveden Hospital service is not known, but operation had started prior to 1st March 1916, when the Local Government (Emergency Provisions) Act 1916 came into effect. One of its provisions was to empower Highways Authorities to restrict the introduction of new bus services to those roads served prior to 1st March 1914, whilst also allowing them to levy a mileage charge on bus operators towards the cost of repairing roads damaged by such 'extraordinary traffic'. Although the Reading Branch was in fact permitted to continue with most of its services (some being subject to a mileage charge), the Cliveden service was ordered to be discontinued. However, public pressure on the Local Authority led to the reinstatement of the service after only a matter of days, and it was thereafter allowed to continue without mileage charges for the remainder of the war years in recognition of its importance in linking the hospital with the town.

The other new service based on Maidenhead was a $10^1/2$ mile route from Cookham to Windsor via Maidenhead. The section between Windsor and Maidenhead had previously been served by the 'London General' company but the service had been withdrawn as a wartime casualty in November 1914. Under the circumstances the LGOC had agreed to let BAT commence its own service over the route, the new service being of some benefit to the LGOC with its connecting services at Windsor. The route commenced in early March 1916 but the precise date has remained illusive.

From 1st March 1916 the Reading to Sunningdale service was extended $2^1/2$ miles onwards at its eastern end to reach Virginia Water, but the Branch was forced under the 1916 Act to withdraw the extension by October that year. The other route abandoned sometime between March and June 1916 was the Wallingford to Abingdon service, though it is unclear as to whether it was discontinued due to poor receipts or in order to conserve declining fuel stocks. The Reading, Arborfield and Wokingham service fell victim to the shortage of fuel and had ceased by 26th February 1916, Special buses did, however, continue to run between Reading and Arborfield at the request of the military throughout the war years.

Although the situation with vehicles had been eased by the arrival of the Belsizes, the acute shortage of drivers continued to be a handicap.

Another factor affecting the buses in the early months of 1916 was the severe weather conditions. During February and March there were very heavy snowstorms in the Thames valley, whilst the 'Great Blizzard' that came with them brought many large trees down across the roads. One BAT bus was damaged by a falling branch during March as it made its way from Wallingford to Reading near Purley but, although the roof was holed and several windows broken, the 10 passengers and crew escaped unharmed. Following on from the snowstorms came exceptionally bad spring flooding, with operations from Maidenhead being particularly badly disrupted. Even without all this, the operation of those early vehicles during the wintertime caused great practical problems. None were fitted with self-starters, so up to 3 men would have to be employed on the large extension tube which was fitted to the starting handle in order to coax the cold engines into life, whilst the lack of anti-freeze solution meant that all radiators had to be drained at night and the water kept in hay-boxes to prevent it freezing overnight.

As already mentioned many of the local roads lacked a tarred surface, and of course it cannot be denied that the arrival of the heavy buses did not help matters at all! Inevitably there was some friction from time-to-time between the Company and the Highways Department of Berkshire County Council, particularly as the latter could find neither the money or the manpower to make good the damage due to the war.

Recruitment of drivers still posed a problem during the first half of 1916 and Mr Homer made strenuous efforts to attract more men above the age then being taken for military service. As part of this campaign a number of men were found lodgings, either at the Caversham Road premises or elsewhere in Reading and Maidenhead, suggesting that they were brought in from outside the area - though it is not known if any were already employees of BAT/BET. Conductors were less difficult to recruit, particularly as a number of the ladies soon had other relatives joining them 'on the back', whilst a number duly also found their future husbands amongst the ranks of the drivers!

Some concern was voiced by BAT management that Graham Homer himself might be called up for military service as the prospects for the early end to the war faded. It was decided that, should that occur, Sidney Garcke would have to give up a considerable amount of his time to managing the Reading Branch, whilst his other interests in 'East Kent' etc. would have to be taken over by other members of the Board.

Meanwhile, the BAT-associated 'Aldershot & District' company had commenced a service between Reading and Aldershot on 1st March 1916 in order to link up with the 'Thames valley system'. Three journeys were operated on weekdays and Saturdays (with one less on Sundays), and the service provided a valuable connection both for the two towns and the operators concerned. Arrangements were soon made for parcels traffic brought into Reading by the buses of A&D or the local Branch to be taken to its ultimate destination by the established Tramways Parcels Service via its office which was situated close to where the buses stopped in St. Mary's Butts.

A further pair of Belsizes, registered DP 1794 (?) and DP 1795, took to the road in July 1916 but, unlike the previous examples, these carried newly-built 26-seat rear-entrance bus bodies constructed by Brush.

The situation with both vehicles and drivers had improved by the summer of 1916, but unfortunately that was not true of the fuel crisis. Experiments were undertaken using a mixture of paraffin and petrol in an effort to eke out the rations allocated to the Branch by the Ministry of Munitions, but as the situation deteriorated more, some service cuts became inevitable. Some routes lost a few journeys, whilst others had their days of operation reduced. Fortunately though, the Branch was able to maintain most of its operations - though A&D had to abandon its service to Reading from 18th December 1916

However, to return to the events of the summer months, July 1916 saw the 'British' buses making their contribution to the success of " the biggest tea party ever held". The idea was that of an Australian lady who wanted to entertain the convalescent troops and who had obtained permission from the King to hold the event in Windsor Great Park. Some 20,000 military personnel and volunteer helpers were brought into the park from the numerous local hospitals and all manner of conveyances were requisitioned in order to transport them (including boats from Cliveden to Windsor).

During the early part of October 1916 Mr Homer was approached to help the military in another way. By then the Royal Flying Corps had established a number of training centres in various buildings within Reading, and their local Commanding Officer asked if the Company would be in a position to provide buses to transport the trainees and their instructors between the various halls. As all of the proposed routes were wholly within the Reading Borough, Mr Homer first asked the Council if they would be agreeable to the operations. The Council acknowledged that its trams could neither cope with the additional traffic or provide a convenient means of travel between the halls, so the necessary permission was forthcoming. 4 routes were set up to meet the needs of the RFC, whilst the further involvement with the military helped to secure better allocations of petrol. The routes were:-

No. 1 - St Patricks Hall to Drill Hall via Northcourt Avenue, Christ-church Road, Whitley Crescent, Whitley Street, Southampton Street, Bridge Street and St. Mary's Butts.

No. 2 - St Patricks Hall to Drill via Northcourt Avenue, Redlands Road, London Road, Crown Street, Southampton Street, Bridge Street and St. Mary's Butts.

No. 3 - Wantage Hall to Kings Hall via Upper Redlands Road, Redlands Road, Watlington Street and Kings Road.

No. 4 - Wantage Hall to Yeomanry Riding School via Upper Redlands Road, Redlands Road, London Road, Crown Street, Southampton Street, Bridge Street and Castle Street.

Approval was given for the above routes on condition that only RFC personnel were carried and that the vehicles were hired by the military rather than fares being payable on the buses. Initial permission was granted until the end of January 1917, but that was duly renewed until the end of July of that year. At first the RFC routes called for 7 buses, resulting in some vehicles having to be borrowed from elsewhere in BAT, but by December demand had subsided and only 3 were required.

The influx of Belsizes had actually been continuing, but it had been decided not to put all of the additional chassis to work at Reading due to the petrol shortage and the unlikelihood of obtaining further drivers.

Some 8 chassis were therefore re-sold (at a profit!) without being used - 2 of them going to the British Red Cross in December 1916.

During November 1916 the final pair of Belsizes to be placed in service arrived in the shape of DP 1826 and 1827, and they had new Brush bodies similar to the previous two. Their arrival resulted in the withdrawal of the 3 remaining Leylands (HE 8, 9 and 12), all of which returned to 'Barnsley & District'.

As the year closed on 1916 it did so on one of mixed fortunes for the Branch, and right towards the close it suffered its first fatal accident involving the buses. A 75-year old lady who was rather deaf fell victim to the bus on a foggy night at Twyford. The accident occurred on Tuesday 27th December as the bus was proceeding from Maidenhead to Reading showing only sidelights due to the Lighting Order, and under those conditions neither the old lady or the driver perceived the presence of the other until it was too late.

However, despite the continued difficulties wrought by the wartime situation, the Branch had still managed to improve its patronage during 1916 and had carried 485,646 passengers over a total of 245,131 miles.

Petrol rationing bit even harder during the early days of 1917, and the January timetable shows that services between Reading and Wallingford were reduced to operate on Tuesdays, Thursdays, Saturdays and Sundays only. Connections could still be made with the 'City of Oxford' buses for Oxford on most days, though its service did not go to Wallingford on Thursdays at that time.

During February 1917 the situation with fuel became so acute that the whole of the Cookham, Maidenhead and Windsor service had to be withdrawn. The precise date is not known, but the public announcement appeared in the local press on the 14th of that month. A number of the buses were fitted with special carburretors in order to improve performance when running on a petrol and paraffin mix in an effort to keep the wheels turning.

Also withdrawn in the early months of 1917 was the 1 mile section of route between Riseley Common and Swallowfield, whilst the Cliveden service had alternate journeys placed on a Tuesdays, Thursdays, Saturdays and Sundays-only basis.

Early in 1917 part of the Caversham Road garage was turned over to the production of shells for the Ministry of Munitions, whilst exceptionally heavy war-related traffic was causing havoc, with the roads south of Reading and Swallowfield becoming so bad in places that the Highways Department found it necessary to place red warning lights to mark where the deeper of the ruts lay!

To add to the Company's difficulties, the local population had been swelled quite considerably by the influx of people who had left London in fear of airborne attacks, so demand for bus services was greater than ever. It did all it could to oblige those who wanted to travel, but its helpfulness led to its being summoned to appear in court at Reading on charges of overcrowding in August 1917. 2 separate counts of such activities were cited before the court, one concerning a 26-seater carrying 41 adults and 5 children on the Swallowfield route, and the other referring to another 26-seater noted carrying 35 adults and a number of children in the Wokingham Road on a journey in from Sunningdale. Mr Homer told the court of the great difficulties being faced by the Company in trying to match demand with very few drivers and less and less fuel. During the course of the hearing it was noted that the Corporation Tramways were also the subject of routine over crowding but that the Borough Police (who were paid by the Corporation) seemed willing to overlook that. The outcome was that BAT had to pay costs, but were otherwise let off with a warning in recognition of the good work it was doing in very difficult circumstances.

After this had happened Graham Homer did try to allay any public anxiety about the buses ability to meet the anticipated demand of the forthcoming Bank Holiday by promising to lay on extra services wherever possible. In order to achieve this several sleeve-engined Daimler double-deckers were sent down from Camden Town to help out at the Branch from late August until about October 1917.

Further eastwards the buses were actually publically praised in the local press for 'incredible overloading' during the very busy Bank Holiday fete held at the Cliveden Hospital, after long queues built up for the homeward journey. Unlike the Reading garage, there were only the bare minimum of spare buses at Maidenhead, so the crews just had to run a continuous shuttle service carrying as many people as could be crammed on until all were once again home!

Also in response to public demand, a new facility came into effect sometime in late summer 1917. This took the form of a 13 $^{1}/2$ mile 'special' between Reading and the Berkshire Lunatic Asylum at Moulsford, and it was operated on the first and third Thursdays of each month for the benefit of visitors to the increasing number of patients transferred there following the conversion of a number of institutions into military hospitals. The bus left St Mary's Butts at 1.15 pm, arriving at the Asylum an hour later, and returning from there at 4.45 pm. Although no return fares were generally available on the buses such fares were issued in respect of this service - according to one driver this was to ensure that no escapees were carried back on the bus!

The staff of the Branch had all worked extremely hard to ensure that some progress had been achieved despite the difficulties, and it was fitting that the first Annual Supper should be held on Friday 7th September 1917 to mark their achievements. By the nature of the business itself, it was not possible to start the proceedings until all the buses had been tucked away for the night, but the 10.30 pm reservation at Bond's Restaurant in West Street, Reading was well attended. Mr Homer led the toast to future progress and went on to read a letter from Sidney Garcke praising all their efforts.

With regard to the terminus arrangements in Reading, it should be noted that St. Mary's Butts was laid out somewhat differently in those days. Whereas today the whole length of it is a good width, at that time the northern end was quite constricted by buildings. At the southern end things were much the same as they are today, though the through traffic (and trams) used only the roadway between the central island and the churchyard wall, the other side from the island playing host to parked carts etc. It was on this same side that the buses found a suitable niche in the corner formed where the buildings jutted out to narrow the northern end of the road. However, as services built up it was necessary to park some buses opposite the old fire station and even in the middle of the road. This was, of course, adjacent to the tram tracks and, on Thursday 13th September 1917, a bad collision occurred between one of the buses and a tram. The bus was quite badly damaged, but fortunately none of the passengers on either conveyance were injured.

Towards the end of the summer of 1917 the petrol situation nationwide became more desparate and led to BAT considering the use of alternative fuels such as coal-gas. More locally there were also some developments along those lines, with the Maidenhead Gas Company noting at its Annual General Meeting the successful use of coal-gas for bus operations elsewhere in the country. It was also stated that its use locally might bring about the reinstatement of the much missed Cookham, Maidenhead and Windsor service. Meanwhile, in Reading itself, Vincent's led the way by converting one of their taxicabs to run on coal-gas early in October 1917. The vehicle had a roof-mounted gas-bag and was capable of running for about 18 miles on one fill.

BAT instructed its Branches to utilise coal-gas wherever practical, and the Reading Branch organised itself for extensive gas operation towards the end of 1917. Filler points consisting of modified lamp standards were arranged with the relevant local gas companies at Hosier Street (adjacent to St. Mary's Butts) in Reading, at the Maidenhead garage and at Sunningdale. Supplies were metered via special valves fitted to the lamp standards and the gas passed through a long flexible pipe into a large canvas bag mounted on the roof of the bus. These bags were boarded in around the sides and tied down to keep them under control, but it was not unknown for a half-empty one to sag down over the body sides or even for one to break free in windy weather! The boarding was soon taken up as advertising space by 'McIlroy's' (who were the main department store chain locally), and therefore provided a little additional revenue. Each bag contained approximately 500 cubic feet of gas but, as this was only equivalent to about 2 gallons of petrol, refilling had to take place at the end of most journeys. The bags themselves were manufactured and supplied by Barton Bros. of Beeston, the pioneer bus operators who also did much towards the acceptance of coal-gas as a means of propulsion.

All but one of the services had been converted to gas operation by the beginning of 1918, but even this ray of hope did not result in the unlimited

Posed outside the Caversham Road premises, this August 1915 view shows the original pair of Leyland buses (HE 11 and 12) complete with route boards for the first service.

Leyland HE 8 halted outside the "Bull" at Riseley on the service from Reading sometime in 1916. Note the open seats at the front and the ladder to the rack on the roof. For some reason, the electric side-lamps have been replaced by acetylene.

This winter 1915 view shows Leylands HE 9 and 10 at St Mary's Butts ready to depart for Swallowfield and Wokingham. Charlie Hampton leans on the mudguard of HE 9, whilst the other driver wears a distinctly military-style greatcoat and the lady conductors are in the typical attire provided for them.

One of the "HE" batch of Leylands stands at the Wellington Monument in 1916 on the summer Sundays extension of the Riseley Common route.

This tranquil scene with Belsize DP 1657 on the Bath Road near the 'Seven Stars' at Knowl Hill provides an indication of both the surface and quietness of the road in those days.

Seen inside the Caversham Road garage are Tilling-bodied Belsize DP 1659 and the chassis of M 7740, one of the Macclesfield Branch Belsize buses in for overhaul.

Freshly painted for service (but lacking any lights), Belsize DP 1756 clearly shows the livery and fleetname used at the Branch. Windscreen wipers were unknown then - note how the driver's window opens for fresh air or to allow him to see on wet days.

Just west of Pangbourne, Belsize DP 1795 makes its way to Streatley and Wallingford. No other wheeled traffic is in sight, unless the lady with the pram is included in that category!

A Brush official photo taken just prior to delivery, complete with unlettered route boards. Compare this view of DP 1827 with that of Tilling-bodied DP 1756 - both bodies were based on the BAT design of the period but there are many detailed differences.

Belsize DP 1827 halts at Ascot High Street on its way from Sunningdale to Reading. Note the total absence of other motor traffic!

Whilst the driver pops into the grocers shop, Graham Homer snaps Brush-bodied Belsize DP 1826 in the sunshine of April 1918 at Peppard Common. Leaning on the mudguard is Bob Hepburn with Homer's son beside him, whilst Mrs Homer stands to the right of the lady conductor.

Belsize DP 1826 drops off passengers at the "Bull" at Riseley. The sides of the bus are covered in dust from the unmade road, whilst in winter the same road was notable for its rutted and muddy condition.

Part of the staff in 1918. Graham Homer and Mrs Homer are flanked at the front by the travelling Inspector and Bob Hepburn, whilst behind them are some of the ladies who acted as conductors and a group of the drivers including tall Charlie Hampton.

Belsize DP 1827 leaves the forecourt of Sunningdale Station for the return journey to Reading.

The old Bracknell High Street is the setting for this view of Belsize DP 1827 taken in 1916 as the bus travelled through from Sunningdale.

On its way from Sunningdale to Reading, Belsize DP 1827 passes Wokingham Town Hall in this 1916 view.

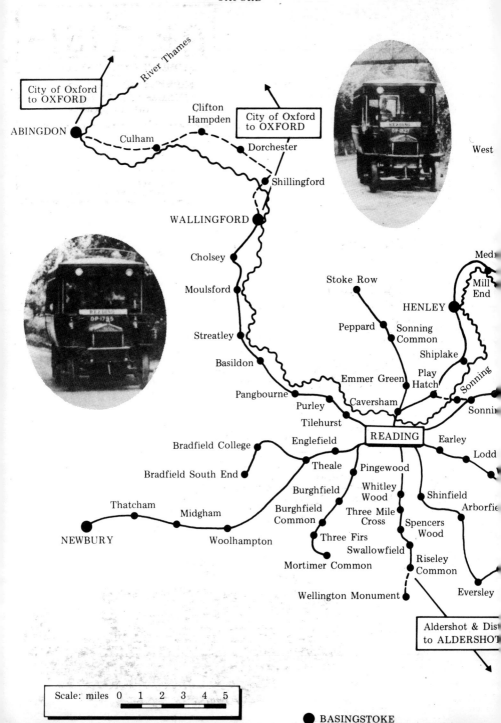

OXFORD

River Thames

City of Oxford
to OXFORD

ABINGDON

Culham

Clifton
Hampden

City of Oxford
to OXFORD

Dorchester

Shillingford

WALLINGFORD

Cholsey

Moulsford

Streatley

Basildon

Pangbourne

Purley

Tilehurst

Englefield

Bradfield College

Bradfield South End

Theale

Thatcham

Midgham

NEWBURY

Woolhampton

Burghfield

Burghfield
Common

Three Firs

Mortimer Common

Stoke Row

Peppard

Sonning
Common

HENLEY

Shiplake

Emmer Green

Play
Hatch

Caversham

READING

Pingewood

Whitley
Wood

Three Mile
Cross

Swallowfield

Wellington Monument

Earley

Shinfield

Spencers
Wood

Riseley
Common

Med

Mill
End

Sonning

Sonni

West

Lodd

Arborfie

Eversley

Aldershot & Dis
to ALDERSHOT

Scale: miles   0   1   2   3   4   5

BASINGSTOKE

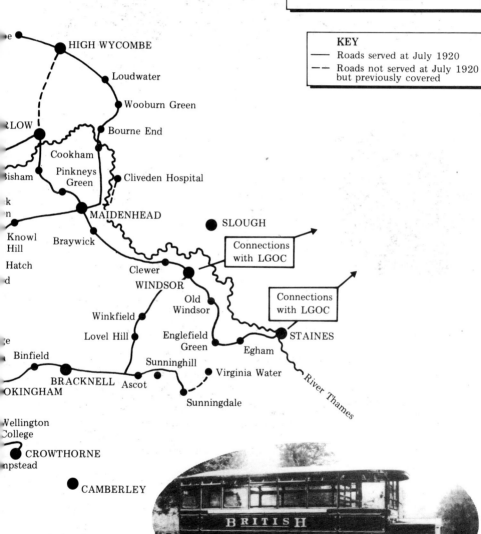

THE BRITISH

AUTOMOBILE TRACTION Co. Ltd.

SERVICES OF THE READING
(THAMES VALLEY BRANCH)
1915 to 1920

KEY

— Roads served at July 1920

- - - Roads not served at July 1920
but previously covered

HIGH WYCOMBE

Loudwater

Wooburn Green

Bourne End

RLOW

Cookham

Bisham

Pinkneys
Green

Cliveden Hospital

k

n

MAIDENHEAD

Knowl
Hill

Braywick

SLOUGH

Connections
with LGOC

Hatch

d

Clewer

WINDSOR

Old
Windsor

Connections
with LGOC

STAINES

Winkfield

Lovel Hill

Englefield
Green

Egham

e

Binfield

Sunninghill

Virginia Water

River Thames

BRACKNELL Ascot

OKINGHAM

Sunningdale

Wellington
College

CROWTHORNE

npstead

CAMBERLEY

BRITISH

-PL-

A 1919 view of the Maidenhead staff and some of its allocation of Thornycroft J-type buses showing (left to right) T6 (DP 2116), T7 (DP2117), T1 (DP 2111), T4 (DP 2114) and T9 (DP 2119).

Seen outside the 'White Hart' in St Mary's Butts at Whitsun 1919 is T5 (DP 2115) bound for Henley and Marlow and carrying an ex-Belsize Tilling body still with boards for retaining the gas-bag. Behind it is similar bus T3 (DP 2113) which is bound for Maidenhead.

Another Whitsun 1919 view at St Mary's Butts, this one shows T8 (DP 2118) with its Tilling body still sporting the gas-bag boards and appropriately with McIlroy's store in the background. Note the ladder for access to the roof and the use of posters in the windows to advertise services and excusions.

Parked in the centre of the roadway at St Mary's Butts, this unidentified member of the Birch-bodied 259-63, 275 batch (DP 2123 to 2128) was photographed in 1919 shortly after entering service.

T19 (DP 2129) was a Thornycroft J which carried a secondhand Bayley "charabus" body making it less vulnerable to the vagaries of the British climate than the conventional charabanc.

T20 (DP 2130) also had a secondhand body, but this Harrington example was of the conventional canvas-hooded charabanc style with full-width seating and a door to each row.

Although actually taken in 1922 (at the Somerset Place garage in Reading), this photo provides an interesting comparison between 16 (DP 2125) on the left, with its low style of bonnet and front-entrance Brush body and 34 (DP 2606) with the higher bonnet height usually found on WD chassis combined with one of the old Tilling bodies.

The 6 Birch bodies built in 1919 were to the basic BAT pattern but showed some detailed differences in window arrangements. DP 2126 was then carrying fleet No. T 16 when posed for this photo by the river at Caversham.

Two views of "Pullman" saloon 336 (DP 2597) taken when new. These Brush bodies represented a change of BAT policy in favour of front-entrance layout, and they had a rear smoking compartment. This example was based on one of the ex-War Department Thornycroft J-type chassis and was allocated to Maidenhead, being shown here with boards for the service to Sunningdale via Windsor.

These 2 views taken after 'Thames Valley' was formed give an opportunity to study the detail differences in the Tilling and Brush rear-entrance bodies transferred from Belsizes to the incoming Thornycroft J-type chassis. At the top we have 8 (DP 2118) with a Tilling body and below is a rare view of one of the Brush-bodied Thornycrofts, 11 (DP 2121). 3 of the 4 Brush-bodied examples were later sold to 'Trent'.

Hired from the Camden Town fleet during 1918 was this Daimler CC-type No. 349 (LF 9219). Both views were taken at Wallingford market place. Note the height of the open-top body and the lack of weather protection for the driver. Several of these buses were hired each summer from 1916 to 1918 to help out with the seasonal peak of traffic.

FLEET LIST 1915 - 1920

Bat No.	TV No.	Reg. No.	Chassis Type	Bodywork	New	Acq.	Out
?	-	HE 8	Leyland S8	Brush B27F	5/13	7/15	11/16
?	-	HE 9	Leyland S8	Brush B27F	5/13	7/15	11/16
?	-	HE 10	Leyland S8	Brush B27F	5/13	7/15	4/16
?	-	HE 11	Leyland S8	Brush B27F	5/13	6/15	4/16
?	-	HE 12	Leyland S8	Brush B27F	5/13	6/15	11/16
?	-	DP 1655	Belsize 3-ton	Tilling B26R	9/15		
?	-	DP 1656	Belsize 3-ton	Tilling B26R	9/15		
?	-	DP 1657	Belsize 3-ton	Tilling B26R	9/15		1/19
?	-	DP 1658	Belsize 3-ton	Tilling B26R	9/15		to
?	-	DP 1659	Belsize 3-ton	Tilling B26R	9/15		2/19
?	-	DP 1660	Belsize 3-ton	Tilling B26R	9/15		
?	-	DP 1756	Belsize 3-ton	Tilling B26R	3/16		
?	-	DP 1757	Belsize 3-ton	Tilling B26R	3/16		
?	-	? DP 1794	Belsize 3-ton	Brush B26R	7/16		2/19
?	-	DP 1795	Belsize 3-ton	Brush B26R	7/16		2/19
?	-	DP 1826	Belsize 3-ton	Brush B26R	11/16		2/19
?	-	DP 1827	Belsize 3-ton	Brush B26R	11/16		2/19
244	1	DP 2111	Thornycroft J	Tilling B26R	1/19		4/31
245	2	DP 2112	Thornycroft J	Tilling B26R	1/19		10/28
246	20	DP 2113	Thornycroft J	Tilling B26R	1/19		12/31
247	23	DP 2114	Thornycroft J	Tilling B26R	1/19		12/31
248	5	DP 2115	Thornycroft J	Tilling B26R	1/19		1/29
249	6	DP 2116	Thornycroft J	Tilling B26R	2/19		2/29
250	7	DP 2117	Thornycroft J	Tilling B26R	2/19		10/28
251	8	DP 2118	Thornycroft J	Tilling B26R	2/19		11/29
252	9	DP 2119	Thornycroft J	Brush B26R	2/19		5/23
253	10	DP 2120	Thornycroft J	Brush B26R	2/19		6/23
254	11	DP 2121	Thornycroft J	Brush B26R	2/19		5/23
255	12	DP 2122	Thornycroft J	Brush B26R	2/19		2/29
259	14	DP 2123	Thornycroft J	Birch B26R	4/19		9/28
260	15	DP 2124	Thornycroft J	Birch B26R	4/19		2/29
261	16	DP 2125	Thornycroft J	Birch B26R	4/19		3/29
262	17	DP 2126	Thornycroft J	Birch B26R	4/19		10/28
263	19	DP 2127	Thornycroft J	Birch B32R	7/19		12/29
275	18	DP 2128	Thornycroft J	Birch B32R	7/19		2/29
276	13	DP 2129	Thornycroft J	Bayley ChB28F	5/19		6/31
278	3	DP 2130	Thornycroft J	Harrington Ch28	5/19		11/31
279	21	DP 2377	Thornycroft J	Lorrybus 32	7/19		5/28
295	22	DP 2378	Thornycroft J	Lorrybus 32	8/19		9/29
298	4	DP 2605	Thornycroft J	Tilling B26R	1/20		5/29
310	25	KN 3652	Thornycroft J	LGOC O34ROS	5/19	1/20	6/29
311	26	KN 2873	Thornycroft J	LGOC O34ROS	3/19	1/20	1/29
316	27	DP 2599	Thornycroft J	Tilling B26R	WD	2/20	6/23
336	28	DP 2597	Thornycroft J	Brush B29F	WD	4/20	3/29
337	29	DP 2601	Thornycroft J	Brush B29F	WD	4/20	7/29
338	30	DP 2598	Thornycroft J	Brush B29F	WD	4/20	11/28
339	31	DP 2602	Thornycroft J	Brush B29F	WD	4/20	6/29
340	32	DP 2603	Thornycroft J	Brush B29F	WD	4/20	6/29
341	33	DP 2604	Thornycroft J	3-ton lorry	WD	4/20	5/28
352	24	DP 2600	Thornycroft J	Birch B26R	WD	4/20	2/29
-	34	DP 2606	Thornycroft J	Tilling B26R	8/20		9/28

(Bat Nos. 336–352 bracketed as "order unknown")

NOTES: The BAT Nos. shown are listed against the original registration Nos. carried, whilst the TV Nos. are those allocated in 8/20. Due to body changes etc. these two lists cannot necessarily be cross-referenced. The 'local' fleet Nos. of 1918/9 period are not shown, nor are buses hired from BAT (Camden Town). A further chassis (BAT No. 354) passed to TV but was dismantled in 8/20, its place being taken by that which became TV No. 34. The bodies shown above are those first fitted for service, details of body changes for the period to the end of 8/20 are included in the main text. A number of bodies therefore appear above more than once.

use of the buses, as from January 1918 the Gas Restriction Order limited the amount of gas that could be made available for running motor vehicles!

Mr Homer was particularly concerned that both the vehicles and the crews should have a smart appearence in order to tempt would-be passengers onto the buses. Male employees had white dustcoats for summer use and dark-coloured greatcoats for wintertime, whilst official hats were expected to be worn at all times when on duty. Hat badges were provided, though in the early days they consisted of a mixture of the BET 'magnet' device and other bearing the legend 'British' in even-sized capital letters. The lady conductors had similar types of coats for seasonal use, but their headgear was adapted from wide-brimmed hats to which a ribbon had been added for the fixing of the company badge.

Despite 1917 having been another difficult year, passenger loadings had increased to 571,095, though the mileage had decreased to 215,279 - a clear indication of how much busier the buses had been.

As already mentioned, the Camden Town Branch would some- times help Reading (and other locations) out when difficulties arose. Even so, Reading also did its bit whenever it could, and arrangements were duly made for the regular overhauling of Belsizes from the Macclesfield Branch at the Caversham Road works. On another particular occasion, Graham Homer had to rush a Camden Town Daimler double-decker down to Bournemouth following the mechanical failure of both the buses assigned to the County Gates to Sandbanks service of the fledgling 'Bournemouth & District' company (the forerunner of 'Hants & Dorset').

As a consequence of introducing gas propulsion it proved necessary to revise all the timetables in January 1918 to take into account the need for the refilling of gas containers and reduced performance on the road. Somewhat ironically, there were actually some favourable comments about the gas buses in the local press, particularly relating to the absence of the pungent smell which had accompanied the petrol/paraffin experiments. However the addition of the roof-mounted containers did lead to some problems with overhanging trees etc., and towards the end of January 1918 the Company approached Maidenhead Borough Council about having some of the trees in Grenfell Road lopped to avoid fouling the gas-bags. The Council replied that the easier solution was to re-route the buses rather than to expend on tree cutting, and they instructed BAT for run its buses directly down Castle Hill and the High Street rather than entering the town via Grenfell Road and Queen Street (which had been chosen for its close proximity to the railway station). Incidentally, the main stopping point in that town was the 'Bear Hotel', which was situated just a short way along the Bath Road from the garage and provided an historical link with the mail coaches of a previous era.

On the 13th February 1918 one of the Belsizes was involved in a rather nasty fatal accident at Sonning Bridge at Shepherds Hill on the road between Reading and Twyford, though the bus driver was later exonerated from any blame. As the bus was coming off the bridge, which was itself situated at an angle to the main course of the road in order to carry it over the railway, a cyclist who had been holding onto the back of a van swerved out into the path of the bus. His body and bicycle became so wedged that the front wheel and part of the engine had to be dismantled before it could be disentangled from the bus. It should be noted that although the BAT buses were indeed involved in a small number of accidents in those early years, there was only one occasion when the driver was taken to be at fault - and even that incident might not have led to a fine had the bus not collided with the car of a local magistrate!

Following on from restrictions on petrol and gas came the Lighting, Heating & Power Order of April 1918, which sought to conserve falling stocks of coal by restricting supplies to both domestic users and to the gas companies.

All the same, the 'British' buses in the Thames valley had done well to maintain whatever services they could. Recruitment of crews still presented difficulties in 1918 and it was not unknown for Graham Homer or Bob Hepburn to take a turn behind the wheel at times. Despite the general need for fuel economy however, an experimental limited service was started over the 7 miles between Reading and Peppard Common in April 1918, (possibly to take the place of the 'Peppard & District Motor Service' of Bert Butler which had been withdrawn due to the war?) and this was evidently operated by a bus running on conventional fuel. However, this facility had been discontinued by the following month as not enough fuel was available at Reading.

All BAT vehicles had for some years been allocated a 'book' number for accounting purposes, with each individual chassis and body being numbered separately in the same series. Generally these numbers were not displayed as fleet numbers, and no evidence relating to that practice has come to light prior to 1919 in respect of the Reading Branch. However, in common with several other BAT locations, the Reading Branch did introduce a series of 'local' fleet numbers by the spring of 1918. These were painted on a small disc fixed to the front canopy of the bodywork, but details of those allocated to the Belsizes are unknown.

For May 1918 the timetables of most services were revised and, with some improvement in the petrol situation, it was also found possible to recommence the service between Maidenhead and Windsor with effect from Wednesday 1st May. Indeed, the Branch was publicly praised for the re-opening of that important and popular link between the neighbouring towns, whilst the sentiment was aired that it would hopefully not be too long before the Maidenhead to Cookham section could also be reinstated. The short section of route between Swallowfield and Riseley Common was also put back into operation at that same time.

To recap on the situation as it stood at May 1918, the Branch was operating 6 services as follows:-

Reading to Maidenhead, via Sonning Halt, Twyford, Knowl Hill and Maidenhead Thicket.
Reading to Wallingford, via Tilehurst, Pangbourne, Streatley, Moulsford and Cholsey.

Reading to Sunningdale, via Earley, Winnersh, Wokingham, Binfield, Bracknell and Ascot.
Reading to Riseley Common, via Whitley Wood, Three Mile Cross, Spencers Wood and Swallowfield.
Maidenhead to Cliveden Hospital, via Maidenhead Bridge, Berry Hill and Taplow Court.
Maidenhead to Windsor, via Braywick, Holyport Turn, Fifield Turn and Clewer.

In order to maintain those services 6 buses were required at Reading (2 each for the Maidenhead and Sunningdale routes, and 1 each for the Wallingford and Riseley Common routes), whilst the schedules at Maidenhead called for 1 bus for each of the 2 routes covered. However, despite the 65-minute journey time between Reading and Maidenhead, there had been no attempt to involve the latter garage in the operation of the service, resulting in the first bus from Maidenhead being the rather late 10.15 am departure. At that same point in time Reading had 11 drivers and 12 conductors (all but 1 of the latter being female), whereas Maidenhead had 3 drivers and 2 lady conductors.

It should be noted that regular timetable leaflets had been issued since the early days of the Branch, but the May 1918 issue was the first to feature a route map. Apart from showing the services operated by the Branch, it also clearly indicated where those services met the routes of the neighbouring other large operators. Connections could be made with the widespread 'London General' routes at Windsor, with 'City of Oxford' at Wallingford, and with 'Aldershot & District' at Riseley Common (A&D having reinstated their service to that point from Aldershot).

Apart from the buses required to cover the scheduled services there were also numerous occasions when extra buses were required during the summer months, whilst most of the annual overhaul work generally took place over the winter months. With less leisure time on their hands in those days, people flocked out to local beauty spots at weekends and Bank Holidays, whilst local events of all kinds always attracted good attendances. The summer of 1918 was a particularly busy period for the Branch, with the good weather tempting many of those who were wearying of the continuing warfare out into the sunshine of the Thames valley. After an exceptionally busy Whitsun, Graham Homer had to seek help from Camden Town for the months ahead. A pair of Daimler CC-type double-deckers (including No. 349, LF 9219) were sent down to take up duties at Reading towards the end of July in time for the school holidays, and were generally found on the Wallingford route.

Extra buses had to be laid on in connection with a large fete held at 'Highlands' in Spencers Wood during July 1918, when an all day shuttle service was in operation. A similar garden fete at Hartley Court, Three Mile Cross also attracted large crowds later that month and extra journeys had to be slotted into the normal timetable to cope with the demand.

With the onset of autumn it proved possible to return the Camden Town Daimlers to London as passenger levels took their usual seasonal downturn, leaving the maintenance staff time to attend to the winter overhaul programme.

On the 11th November 1918 the First World War finally came to an end. As far as the 'Reading Thames valley Branch' (as it had latterly come to be known) was concerned, that meant fresh thoughts of future expansion. Much preparatory work was under- taken that winter towards the goal of enlarging operations during 1919 as soon as further buses and drivers could be obtained.

During December 1918 the suggestion had come from the public (via the columns of the 'Maidenhead Advertiser') that consideration should be given to diverting the Maidenhead to Windsor service to take in Bray village. It was argued that such a deviation would be of great benefit to the residents there but would only add some 5 minutes to the overall journey time. However, at that particular point in time, the roads around Bray were acknowledged to be some of the worst in condition in the whole of the county, so it was not considered practical to run buses along them.

1918 had been an exceptionally busy year for the Branch and, although the mileage operated had only risen by 5% to 233,216, there had been an increase in passengers carried by 22% to 699,496. At the Annual Dinner held in December of that year Sidney Garcke (who was about to stand down as Managing Director of the Branch due to other commitments) told the guests that a large number of new buses were on order for delivery during 1919, whilst it was also hoped to start regular coastal excursions during the next 'season'.

With the war now over, Thornycrofts of Basingstoke were at long last able to fulfil the BAT order for J-type chassis for use at the Branch. The original order for 20 chassis started to arrive during January 1919, with 5 examples becoming BAT Nos. 244 to 248 (DP 2111 to 2115), these being followed by 7 more in February which became Nos. 249 to 255 (DP 2116 to 2122). The first 8 received the 26-seat Tilling bodies from the Belsizes that they replaced, whereas the last 4 were given the newer Brush 26-seat bodies from the later Belsizes. Although it is evident that the BAT numbers were actually displayed as bonnet numbers for a time during the 1919/20 period 'local' series fleet numbers were allocated and these first 20 vehicles were given Nos. T1 to T20 - the 'T' apparently indicating 'Thames valley Branch'.

In the meantime orders were placed with Birch Bros. of Kentish Town for the refurbishment of 2 secondhand charabanc bodies and for the construction of 6 new bus bodies, the work commencing in February 1919.

The arrival of the Thornycroft buses led to the reinstatement ('by popular public demand') of 3 journeys per day between Reading and Peppard Common from Saturday 8th March 1919. 4 more chassis were sent from Thornycrofts during April 1919 and took the first quartet of the Birch rear-entrance 26-seater bus bodies to become BAT Nos. 259 to 262 (DP 2123 to 2126). Their arrival allowed the introduction of the first completely new postwar route on Tuesday 15th April, when the 17 mile long Reading to Marlow service came into operation via Shiplake, Henley,

Hambleden Turn and Medmenham. The service competed with E.G. Venn-Brown's 'Venture' service over the road between Reading and Henley, leading him to diversify his operations to tap custom from villages not covered by the 'British' buses. The new through service provided a useful link between the 3 towns, and it was covered by one Maidenhead-based bus which ran dead to take up the route at Marlow. During that same month the Company sought permission from Berkshire County Council to allow it to run a bus service between Maidenhead and Marlow, and such permission was shortly forthcoming on the basis of a payment per car mile being made.

Other proposed new routes were also the subject of discussion during April 1919, though difficulties arose regarding their actual implementation. A proposed Maidenhead to Henely service was aired in the local press at the end of that month in an effort to gain public support for the Company's application to run over roads beyond those previously covered by the withdrawn GWR bus service between Maidenhead and Hurley. The newspaper item also stated that the introduction of such a service would be of great benefit to golfers, who would then be able to reach the Temple Golf Links from every part of Berkshire!

Berkshire C.C. gave permission for the use of the roads under its care between Maidenhead and Marlow, whilst Cookham Rural District Council followed suit on 23rd April 1919. The service actually started by 30th April and it followed a $5\,^1/2$ mile route through Furze Platt, Pinkneys Green and Bisham. However, although Cookham RDC was at first happy to allow the use of its roads without payment of fees, it soon changed its mind and decided to apply to the Minister of Transport to allow it to impose a mileage charge. In the meantime it did allow the service to continue and, by May 1919, the link between Maidenhead and Cookham village itself had also been renewed.

During the week commencing Monday 15th June 1919 two further new services were started. The first was between Reading and Mortimer Common (some $8\,^1/2$ miles) and the other ran between Reading and Bradfield (South End), some 10 miles from Reading and routed via the famous Bradfield College. Both services were to places already served by Mr Venn-Brown's routes, though the BAT buses ran daily whereas his were more akin to the pattern associated with the carriers market-day operations. Whether any serious competition with Venn-Brown was deliberately embarked upon is unclear, but he continued to run a number of routes in the area until finally selling out in 1928. Not that it was all plain sailing for BAT, as the introduction of the Bradfield service soon brought forth complaints from Bradfield RDC concerning damage to the roads, whilst such sentiments were echoed more generally by the County Council as a number of their roads were suffering from the addition of new bus traffic. All the same, during the same week as the two new services were started, an additional journey was added to the Maidenhead to Cookham route, whilst the Company also stated that a much improved timetable for that service would come into operation on 1st July.

The 2 outstanding chassis earmarked for the remaining 2 bodies due from Birch arrived early in May but, with the approaching charabanc 'season' so close, it was decided to fit them with the pair of renovated bodies intended for that class of work. Both bodies were secondhand (though their origins are unknown), one being a conventional canvas-hooded multi-doorway 28-seater charabanc built by Harrington (of Hove), whilst the other was also a 28-seater but of the less common 'charabus' variety. The latter body was built by Bayley (of Newington Causeway in London) and featured a full-height fixed front windscreen, a solid (but removable) roof, drop-down side sheets for inclement weather and seating arranged in bus-like fashion around a central gangway. Unlike conventional charabancs its nearside body had only 2 functioning doorways, though beading had been added to give the appearance of doorways along the full length of the side. To allow the use of the vehicle with a canvas hood in place of the solid roof the rearmost part of the body was upswept to accommodate the hood when in the down position. However, it is evident from photographs that the vehicle ran with its fixed roof for much (if not all) of the 1919 season, before being converted to full charabanc specification in time for the 1920 season.

Of the two the Bayley-bodied example was the first to take to the road, becoming BAT No. 276 (DP 2129), with the season commencing on Saturday 17th May 1919. It was based at Reading, and initially the advertised excursions only ventured to relatively local destinations. Most were arranged in the form of circular tours, to take in such places as Abingdon and Oxford, Windsor and Virginia Water, Oxford and Henley or Wallingford and Henley, all being run as afternoon outings which left St Mary's Butts at 2.15pm. In the main they were run on Saturdays and Sundays, but some operated on Wednesdays when the half-day closing of the Reading shops took place.

The Harrington-bodied chara became BAT No. 278 (DP 2130) and joined the charabus at Reading at the end of May. Its arrival allowed the scope of the advertised excusions to be widened, the first outings of any real distance being those to Epsom Races for the Derby (4th June) and the Oaks (6th June), whilst Whit Monday 9th June saw the first coastal excusion (to Southsea). Some private hire work was also undertaken during June, the only competition then to be found in Reading being Edwin Venn-Brown's 'Venture' charabanc. Bookings for the excursions could be made at the Caversham Road office, or, more centrally, at the Tramway's Parcels Office in St Mary's Butts.

June 1919 was a very busy month for the two 'charas', with the first postwar Ascot Races and also racing at Newbury, whilst throughout the summer trips were run to most of the races at Windsor, Epsom, Goodwood and Lewes. Loadings on the bus services were also very heavy for the Ascot Races in June, the course having been closed for use by the military since 1915. During early June the Henley Regatta was also well attended and that was marked by a shuttle service of charas and buses from Reading throughout the day and late into the evening.

Although some private hire work had taken the charas to the coast during June, it was not until Sunday 6th July 1919 that a regular weekly coastal excusion became part of the advertised programme. Saturdays and Sundays remained the most popular days for such outings, but other days were also tried in order to gauge the demand, whilst the programme was generally enhanced with the commencement of the school holidays. Indeed, July and August saw much new ground being broken, with the first advertised trips to Burnham Beeches, Bournemouth and Brighton, with Bognor following on in September.

In an effort to promote the excursions, a large watercolour painting of the Harrington chara (local fleet No. T.20) was commissioned and prints were produced for display in the booking office windows. The artist very accurately portrayed the vehicle, and amongst the passengers could easily be discerned Mr & Mrs Homer, their young son and both Emile and Sidney Garcke!

Private hire work built up during the summer of 1919 and it was sometimes necessary to supplement the capacity of T20 and Bayley-bodied T19 with some ordinary service saloons for larger parties. One such job was undertaken on Bank Holiday Monday 25th August, when the two 'charas' were joined by saloons T3 (DP 2113) and T12 (DP 2122) to convey 126 members of the Coley Mission Hall from Reading to Southsea for their annual outing. The event was suitably publicised in the local press - and Graham Homer made sure that a 'British' private hire ad was placed alongside the write-up and photos.

Unfortunately, however, the Reading Borough Police outing to that same destination just 3 days later was dogged with problems. Both T19 and T20 set off for Southsea, but had only reached Swallowfield when one of them developed a small fire under the bonnet. No real damage was done and the driver was able to rectify the fault and carry on with the journey. But the weather also marred the day, and those who had taken seats on the 'charabus' must have appreciated the roof being in place that day!

On the whole though the 1919 'season' was blessed by good weather and, by the end of the advertised excursions towards the close of September, 80 such trips had been operated with a very good level of public support.

A number of alterations and additions were also made to the bus services during the summer months of 1919, many of them coming into effect from 1st July. In general the frequencies of services saw much improvement, whilst at that same time Maidenhead-based buses started to take a hand in the operation of the route from that town to Reading. The Ascot to Sunningdale section of the service from Reading was reduced to just one daily return run, but compensation was forthcoming in the form of a new service between Maidenhead and Sunningdale. That route incorporated the established Maidenhead to Windsor section of the Cookham to Windsor service, and ran on from Windsor to Sunningdale via Winkfield, Lovel Hill and Ascot (covering much the same route as the long-established GWR buses between Windsor and Ascot). Amongst those who took notice of the new services was recently demobilised Frank Williams, who lived near Lovel Hill and who had driven Army lorries during the war years. Attracted by the smart green Thornycroft buses and the prospect of steady employment, he went to work for BAT at the Maidenhead garage and (as was considered unremarkable in those days) he cycled the 9 miles to work and back in all weathers and at unsocial hours. In January 1921 his journey was considerably shortened by his transfer to the Ascot dormy shed at Englemere Farm, and he later then moved to the new garage in Course Road off Ascot High Street in 1924. When Ascot closed in favour of the new garage at Bracknell New Town in 1960 he went there as Depot Inspector, retiring shortly afterwards at the completion of 42 years service.

Also on the 1st July 1919 the Maidenhead to Cookham section became a service in its own right, whilst that date is also believed to have seen the finish of the service to Cliveden Hospital (following the closure of the military hospital), and also the introduction of a new service between Reading and Arborfield Cross via Shinfield.

By August 1919 the single through journey between Reading and Sunningdale had been deleted altogether, though the road between Ascot and Sunningdale still remained covered by the buses from Maidenhead - that service also being extended a short distance to Maidenhead Bridge on summer Sundays in order to give direct access to the riverside.

Berkshire County Council was approached during July 1919 regarding BAT's desire to start up further routes along roads under its care. Services proposed were the Maidenhead to Henley link already noted, a Pangbourne to Theale link, a service between Wokingham and Camberley (to meet 'Aldershot & District'), and other services between Henley, Hurst and Wokingham, Maidenhead, Warfield and Bracknell, Newbury, Kingsclere and Basingstoke, and an extension of the Mortimer Common route onto Silchester and Tadley. Some of these aims were soon to be achieved, whilst others had to wait many years before such routes were covered by the Company.

The progress of the local BAT routes had been noted in many quarters, even resulting in an enquiry from Swindon Corporation as to whether the Company might consider opening a bus link between its town and Reading. In reply, Mr Homer stated that once the Reading to Newbury route had been established some thought would be given to the idea of running such a service - though in the event it was to be over 30 years before the town was reached with the acquisition of 'Newbury & District'.

The 2 outstanding Birch-bodied buses were prepared for service during July 1919 and became BAT Nos. 263 and 275 (DP 2127 and 2128) and bore local fleet numbers T17 and T18. Although originally ordered as 26-seaters, each was fitted out with special gangway seats (for evaluation purposes it is believed), bringing their capacities to 32. The body on T17 was fitted with wooden slatted seats plus gangway seats which dropped down when not in use, whereas T18 was given cushioned seats and tip-up gangway seats.

The above 2 buses completed the original order for 20 J-type chassis, but Thornycrofts were by them in a position to supply chassis quite readily so 3 more were taken during July and August 1919. Whereas the first 20 chassis had been built to the civilian specification (with a reasonably low bonnet height), these additional examples were of the high-bonnetted military pattern and were probably originally part of an order intended for the War Department. The first of them came in July as BAT No. 279 (DP 2377), although a local fleet number may not have been allocated as the Branch was going through a phase of actually using the BAT numbers for vehicle identification. It was closely followed at the start of August by BAT No. 295 (DP 2378), and both of them came complete from Thornycrofts as 'lorrybuses' - i.e. with WD lorry-type bodies to which were fitted rear steps, wood bench seats and a canvas hood. Crude though these may sound, they were not any worse then most vehicles then offered by the carriers services, and even the hard-pressed 'London General' had to accept the use of such vehicles on the streets of the Capital for a brief time. The pair were undoubtably snapped up in order to help the Branch over the busy summer months, though both were rebodied in due course. The third of the additional chassis also arrived during August 1919 and became BAT No. 298 but, as will be seen in due course, it did not enter passenger service for a while.

Therefore the Branch was able to field 22 vehicles for the summer of 1919 compared with only 14 the previous year, whilst plans for even more expansion the following year were put in hand.

Howver, although new chassis could then be readily obtained, the BAT Board decided that it would be desirable to purchase suitable chassis from the large numbers of surplus military vehicles then being sold off relatively cheaply. Chassis of AEC, Daimler and Thornycroft manufacture were particularly favoured, and it is evident that it was decided at an early stage to concentrate certain types in particular fleets. Thornycrofts were already the chosen type for the Reading Branch, doubtless influenced by the fact that the Basingstoke works were only 17 miles away. Sales of the ex-WD vehicles took place at the Slough 'dump' and the close proximity of the Branch ideally placed it to become a purchasing agent for large numbers of chassis destined for use in other BAT fleets in addition to those it earmarked for its own use.

Batches of such vehicles, usually still complete with WD pattern 3-ton lorry bodies, were picked out at the Slough sales and initially taken to the open ground at the rear of the Maidenhead garage before onward delivery to their intended fleet. During the 1919-21 period a large number of AEC's and Daimlers were supplied to the Macclesfield Branch and to 'Northern General', whilst it is also possible that some of the 'Trent' Thornycrofts were selected by the local Branch. 4 Daimler Y-types were sent down to 'Southdown' in the early months of 1920, Graham Homer being on friendly terms with the management there, but the trade was not only a one-way affair as the Branch also handled the sale of numerous redundant Belsize chassis from Macclesfield and Barrow in addition to its own examples of that make. Most of the Belsizes were fitted with the lorry bodies obtained on the ex-WD chassis before being sold locally, but notable amongst the sales were 2 such chassis which went to Reading Corporation Tramways in March 1919 for use as a tower- wagon and as a box-van for the rail welding unit.

The Branch also made some practical use of these additional chassis at times for the collection of bodies from the Birch and Brush coachworks, but it nonetheless stuck steadfastly to the Thornycroft 'J' as its standard vehicle type.

To gain interest and support for further new bus services Graham Homer very skillfully sent a number of 'letters' to the editors of the local papers which, in reality, were nothing other than a free means of advertising! The cause was further aided by a series of suggested local walks in the 'Berkshire Chronicle', all of which originated with a journey by BAT bus. Perhaps Mr Homer had sent the writer a free pass to ensure he sampled the new routes as soon as they came into operation?

Although the link with A&D via Wokingham and Camberley did not come to fruition at that time, the Aldershot company did find itself able to reinstate the full Aldershot to Reading service from 4th September 1919.

Meanwhile, increased activity at Maidenhead led to the widening of the forecourt entrance during July 1919, whilst the Branch service vehicle fleet was increased by the addition of 3 secondhand purchases that summer - a BSA motorcycle and sidecar (BAT No. unknown), a 4-seat Bedford car (No. 240) and a Ford model T box-van (No. 257).

Since its inception the branch had enjoyed good industrial relations, but the general mood in the labour market in the early post-war era was a more militant one as working men sought improvements in pay and conditions in return for their selfless toil during the war years on the land, in the factories and on the battlefields of Europe and beyond. Therefore, during a period of a national rail strike in the autumn of 1919, the BAT drivers at Reading Branch staged a stoppage on Monday 29th September in support of their claim for an additional 10 shillings (50p) per week increase in wages. At that particular time the buses were very busy indeed, as they were carrying many extra passengers who would normally have used the trains, and the management soon held talks with the men which resulted in an amicable settlement and a return to normal working on the following day.

During October 1919 the Peppard Common route was extended northwards by a further 2 miles to Stoke Row. The long-awaited 18 mile Reading to Newbury link finally commenced during the week of 20th October, but it provided only 3 return journeys per day on a route that followed the Bath Road through Theale, Woolhampton and Thatcham.

Also during the week commencing 20th October, the Maidenhead to Marlow service had a number of journeys extended onwards by 5 miles to provide a 3-hour headway between Marlow and High Wycombe. Incorporated within the revised timings were the previously 'dead' runs between Maidenhead and Marlow of the car used for the Marlow to Reading route.

Further route developments took place during December 1919, when a High Wycombe local service commenced on the 1st of that month between Loudwater and West Wycombe. In effect it was a replacement for an early bus service of the 'High Wycombe Omnibus Co.' which had ceased during the war years. However, it must have seemed a worthwhile venture, as its operation entailed an 8 mile 'dead' journey between Maidenhead and Loudwater.

By December 1919 some service cuts were found necessary where routes had not generated sufficient receipts. The Maidenhead, Marlow and High Wycombe route was curtailed at Marlow once again, whereas the Reading to Newbury service was 'temporarily suspended' - both routes then being without buses until the following summer. One of the problems then facing the Company was the continued need to make payments per-car-mile to the Highway Authorities, but hope was in sight that such arrangements (born out of wartime necessity) might soon cease.

Another event of some significance occured on 6th December 1919, when Reading Corporation Tramways commenced its first motorbus operation on a route between Caversham Heights and Tilehurst. As with the tram routes, the BAT buses charged slightly higher 'protective' fares over points served by the buses of both concerns, thereby avoiding any clashes between the Branch and the Corporation.

For the Branch itself 1919 had been a record-breaking year, with 447,000 miles run (an increase over 1918 of 90%) and over 1 million passengers carried.

As 1920 dawned, so the Branch looked forward with optimism to another year of expansion, and a number of new buses were due for entry into service in the spring. Indeed, the increased activity had completely outgrown the office accommodation at the Caversham Road premises, and it was decided to move the Local Head Office to the Maidenhead site in January 1920. That move has led to some historical references to the 'BAT Maidenhead Branch', but that is incorrect as the Branch was by then known as the 'Thames valley Branch'. Because of that move some premises were soon secured at 55 St Mary's Butts, where a small Reading office and a public counter for enquiries and bookings were set up.

On the vehicle front January 1920 saw the arrival of a pair of second J-types, both of which carried double-deck bodies. They had both been new to William Sayers & Sons of Margate and were licenced by him as KN 2873 in March 1919 and KN 3652 in May 1919. The bodies fitted to them were LGOC open-top 34-seat rear open-staircase examples built around 1913 and both vehicles ran for Sayers until they sold their bus services to 'East Kent' in September 1919. Thornycrofts were considered as non-standard stock by 'East Kent', so through the Sidney Garcke connection they were transferred for use at the 'Thames valley' Branch. As it was double-deckers were also non-standard for the Branch, but a suitable use was found for them as will be noted shortly. They were allocated BAT Nos. 310 (KN 3652) and 311 (KN 2873) upon their arrival.

On Friday 6th February 1920 a grand festive evening was arranged for the staff and their guests at Maidenhead Town Hall, where they were treated to a meal and provided with entertainment from within their own ranks. The 140 guests heard of future plans from Graham Homer and Sidney Garcke, whilst the centrepiece of the stage decorations was a model of a 'British' bus made by Mr Slade - detailed finely enough to include the Bridge Street cat!

During the early part of 1920 the Caversham Road offices were taken over by the engineering section, whilst at Maidenhead the garage was extended rearwards to provide additional accommodation for the new cars expected shortly and for the introduction of charabanc operations from that location.

As noted previously, BAT policy directed the use of ex-WD chassis wherever possible, and the Branch acquired 9 J-types from Slough during the early months of 1920. At the same time an order was placed with Brush for 14 29-seater bus bodies of improved design (though only 12 actually found their way to the Branch).

Now, it should be appreciated that, prior to the introduction of the Roads Act 1920 on 1st January 1921, it was not necessary to declare a chassis number in relation to a specific registration number. As the registration plates of buses were often fixed to the bodywork, this often resulted in chassis taking on the identity of the registration carried already by a body transferred to it after overhaul. At the time that the incoming ex-WD chassis were being prepared for use, a number of one-year old J's were also going through the workshops for overhaul. Added to this, there were still certain other vehicles which lacked proper bus bodies, resulting in an interesting period when vehicle identities, bodies and registration numbers became well and truly mixed!

Some use was made of the 2 ex-'East Kent' double-deckers when the Branch broke new ground on Monday 1st March 1920 with a service between Windsor (Castle) and Staines Bridge, with connections for Maidenhead at Windsor. One of the 'deckers was used to assist in tree-cutting duties prior to the service commencing, but the use of the double-deck buses did not please the Chief Constable of Windsor, and he reprimanded the Company for failing to present them for inspection before use. The choice of Staines Bridge as the terminus was made in order to avoid having to run into the strictly controlled Metropolitan Police area on the other side of the river. When the service started it was announced that through buses between Maidenhead and Staines Bridge would soon be introduced, whilst a contemporary press report voiced the hope that buses would soon be running through to central London.

Delivery of the new Brush bodies commenced in April 1920 and they were indeed quite an improvement on the previous examples. 11 of the 29 seats were in a screened 'smoking' compartment at the rear, whilst the entrance was located at the front. Referred to as 'Pullman saloons' by Graham Homer, these vehicles were intended for use on the longer routes and, when demand required it, for excursion work as well.

However, firstly we must turn our attention to the ex-WD chassis which were acquired during the early part of 1920. All were of the standard 3-ton Thornycroft J-type with the higher bonnet specified for military use, and they became BAT Nos. 316, 336, 337, 338, 339, 340, 341, 352 and 354. These 9, together with the unbodied chassis bought earlier from the makers (No. 298)) were allocated registration numbers. DP 2597 to 2606 - but these were neither used exclusively for the 10 chassis, nor were they issued in numerical order. Also, the chassis of 354 was destined not to be run at all, as will be noted in due course.

As the new Brush bodies came into the fleet between April and June 1920 some went straight onto ex-WD chassis and took up registrations DP2597, 2598, 2601, 2602 and 2603. One such body replaced the lorrybus body on DP 2378, and both it and the other lorrybus body were sold to the Macclesfield Branch. Both of the former 'East Kent' double-deckers received new Brush saloon bodies in June, their old bodies going to 'Southdown' for further service. The other new Brush bodies were placed on overhauled cars DP 2115, 2117 and 2125 taking the place of the old Tilling and Birch bodies originally carried by those three. Another car to lose its Tilling body was DP 2114, but in its case the registration plates went with the body and onto the previously unregistered chassis purchased from Thornycroft the year before. When the previous bearer of DP 2114 emerged from overhaul it was fitted with one of the new Brush bodies and given unallocated registration number DP 2605.

In addition to the above, some of the former WD chassis received as the first bodies some of the older overhauled rear-entrance bus bodies, with DP 2600 receiving one of the Birch bodies and DP 2599 one of the Tilling batch. Harrington-bodied chara DP 2130 and Tilling saloon DP2113 had their bodies swapped over during the course of overhauls in May 1920, and the above events provided a wide variety of combination in such a relatively small fleet!

Registration DP 2604 was allocated to an ex-WD chassis which retained its lorry body and ran as a service vehicle until the following spring (when it received a new charabanc body), whilst the 2 other unbodied chassis (DP 2377 and what was intended to become DP 2606) remained so for the meantime.

Cars DP 2122 and 2124 also went in for a body exchange sometime in 1920, leaving DP 2122 with a Birch body and DP 2124 with one of the old Brush rear-entrance type.

To return to other events, the month of May 1920 was an important and busy one for the Branch. The buses had to cope with the vast crowds attending the first post-war 'Royal Counties Show' held at Prospect Park,

Reading, whilst a number of service alterations also came into effect on the 1st of that month. Many were of a minor nature, but more significant was the rearrangement of the services between Maidenhead and Staines and Ascot. Alternate buses from Maidenhead now ran on from Windsor to either Staines Bridge or to Ascot High Street, leaving the Ascot to Sunningdale section to be covered by the service from Reading once again.

During the third week of May 1920 the Company announced to the public that it soon hoped to join its remote Loudwater to West Wycome route with that between Maidenhead to Cookham to provide through services between Maidenhead and West Wycombe as soon as permission could be obtained for the use of the roads - the through route duly commencing on 9th July 1920.

Charabanc excursions recommenced from Reading on Sunday 16th May for the 1920 season, and there was far more emphasis on coastal runs that year. Given the success of the charas during the previous season it is perhaps a little surprising that no further examples were added for the second year of operation. However, as well as the chara trips, a notable additional facility was the regular Mondays-only bus service from Reading to Southsea during August of that year. The service was intended for those passengers who wish to stay at the coast for a week at a time and its operation was handled by the new 'Pullman' saloons, allowing much more luggage to be carried than on the charas. Special weekly return tickets were issued for this service.

Only one chara was allocated to Reading for the 1920 season, though additional picking up points were arranged at Wokingham, Bracknell and Ascot for trips running out in that direction. The other broke new ground when, on Thursday 26th May, it commenced a programme of excursions from Maidenhead to various race meetings, followed by the first coastal run (to Brighton) on Whit Sunday 20th June. Unfortunately, that particular day was a 'wash-out' due to the rain but, despite some problems with the weather that year, bookings were good throughout the season. Additional picking up points were duly arranged at Windsor Castle, Egham and Staines Bridge for excursions travelling in that direction from Maidenhead, whilst the Branch faced virtually no competition in that town at that time. Some competition had started up on Reading from Easter 1920 in the form of small owner-driver outfits, but it did not adversely affect the Company's charas, which spent about half of the week on advertised trips and the remainder available for private hire.

On the bus side, the Reading to Newbury service recommenced on 1st July 1920, with three daily journeys as before, but now worked by a car outstationed at Newbury - but even this attempt to establish the route as a viable proposition failed, and it was again discontinued at the end of the year.

However, the Newbury route was rather exceptional in its failure to attract sufficient custom, and it was Graham Homer's policy to keep the public informed of developments. Apart from numerous letters and press releases, he promoted other practical actions, such as the erection of an illuminated map and timetable case on the front wall of Maidenhead Town Hall which was put in place at the end of June 1920.

On the 29th June 1920 a meeting was held with Wokingham RDC to try to come to agreeable terms over the newly-introduced routes between Reading and Crowthorne (via Arborfield, Eversley and Finchampstead) and between Crowthorne and Wokingham. Temporary permission was granted for the continuation of the services, but the RDC would in the meantime be consulting with Berkshire CC to determine an appropriate mileage charge to be paid by the Company. BCC urged WRDC to press the Minister of Transport to uphold a claim for 3 pence per car mile - particularly in view of the Company's recent success in getting the charge in relation to the (better surfaced) Maidenhead to Marlow road reduced from 3 pence to 2 pence. The wrangling continued for some time before a settlement could be offered. In the meantime the buses continued to run, those on the Crowthorne to Wokingham route having a very tight squeeze under the railway arch in Finchampstead Road - a feat not possible in gas-bag days!

Anyway, despite some occasional setbacks, the Branch had managed to largely fulfil its aim of establishing a bus network in the mid-Thames valley region, and the time therefore came for BAT to set up a separate company to continue those developments. The title 'The Thames Valley Traction Co. Ltd.' was chosen and the Head Office continued to be at the Maidenhead garage. Graham Homer and his staff continued to fulfil their respective functions, though it was decided to appoint an Engineer in order to free Mr Homer to concentrate his efforts on the management and development of the Company. Mr J W Dally was appointed as Acting Secretary before becoming Company Secretary, whilst the first Chairman was appropriately Sidney Garcke.

Both BET and Tillings were keen to develop their various bus interests throughout the country and had decided to co-operate rather than compete. Tillings therefore took a hand in the formation of 'Thames Valley', though they had only a 14% stake compared with the 86% of BET when the new Company came into being on 10th July 1920.

At its formation 'Thames Valley' took control of a route network of 147 miles which had already stretched outwards to serve a wide area. Services from Reading ran to Maidenhead; to Pangbourne, Streatley and Wallingford; to Riseley Common; to Sunningdale via Wokingham, Bracknell and Ascot; to Eversley, Crowthorne and Wokingham; to Peppard and Stoke Row; to Marlow via Henley; to Newbury via Thatcham; to Mortimer Common and to Bradfield South End. Services based on Maidenhead ran to Ascot or Staines Bridge (both via Windsor); to Marlow; and to West Wycombe via Cookham, Loudwater and High Wycombe.

Apart from the above routes, many other connections could be made with the services of other operators, whilst a list of settlements up to 2 1/2 miles of the line of the routes was included in the timetable booklets - most people thinking little of such a walk in those days. A good network of

31

parcels agents had also been set prior to 1920, and this continued to expand as further services were added.

With regard to its relations with other large neighbouring concerns, it should be noted that BAT had already formulated territorial understandings with both 'Aldershot & District' and 'London General'. However, when the new company came to clarify the position, Mr Pick of the LGOC pointed out that 'Thames Valley' would be obliged to withdraw from the Loudwater to West Wycombe and Egham to Staines roads should the 'General' decide to run services there.

On the vehicle side 'Thames Valley' inherited 34 Thornycroft J-type chassis and 33 bodies built by Tilling (8 rear-entrance buses), Brush (4 rear-entrance and 12 front-entrance buses), Birch (6 rear-entrance buses), Bayley (1 charabanc), by Harrington (1 charabanc) together with one WD 3-ton lorry body. Full details are shown in the fleet list.

To take charge of this growing fleet came Basil Sutton, who took up the appointment of Engineer on 1st August 1920. Mr Sutton was a man given to meticulous detail, and shortly after his arrival he allocated fleet numbers to all the vehicles and also separate series of numbers for bodies and engines. These numbers allowed him to keep accurate records of the units covered and, most fortunately, they also provided a very comprehensive archive for the study of the early Thames Valley fleet! The exact allocation of fleet numbers is shown in the fleet list.

To return to the services, the poor state of some sections of the road between Crowthorne and Wokingham led to the withdrawal of that route during the last week of July 1920 - that being before word had come from the Minister concerning the appeals of both the RDC and the Company over mileage charges.

As noted above, one of the J-type chasis (BAT No. 354) was without a body at the time of transfer. This particular chassis had not been run and, at the end of July 1920, it was decided to dismantle it for spare parts. During August a new J-type was obtained from Thornycrofts to take its place, and this then received one of the old Tilling 26-seat bus bodies and the registration DP 2606 (which had originally been intended for 354).

Once formed, the new Company was ready to embark on its expansion throughout the exciting era of the '20's and '30's. Between them, Messrs Dally, Homer and Sutton possessed the wide range of skills necessary to see the Company through these interesting times and onwards during the dark days of the war years. All continued to serve the 'Valley well until their respective retirements in 1957, 1943 and 1956 and there is little doubt that each stamped his own mark on the development of 'Thames Valley' to ensure its efficient service to the public and the smart condition of its fleet.